Role-play German

Peter Willig

Lecturer in Education with specific reference to
Teaching of German
Faculty of Education, University of Birmingham

Susanne Bryant

Tutor, Translator, Examiner in German

**Adapted from Role-play practice: French
by Tony Whelpton and Daphne Jenkins**

Longman

To the teacher

This is the companion German version of the French book '*Role-play practice: French*' by Tony Whelpton and Daphne Jenkins. The authors hope that it will provide much-needed help to both teachers and pupils in an area of German language-teaching and testing that is growing rapidly and, with the GCSE examinations, is likely to grow even more.

There is a considerable shortage of suitable material in role-play practice available to schools, since Examining Boards have in general published only a limited number of tests used in past examinations.

One of the principal aims of this book is to make good this deficiency. Although the situations included in the volume have not themselves been used in any public examinaton, the authors have had between them well over fifteen years' experience of devising, conducting and assessing such material for several examining bodies. The level, format and style of the situations all follow closely those adopted by the vast majority of Examining Boards, although in certain instances emphases obviously vary. However, it must be stressed that the views and opinions expressed in the book are those of the authors themselves and are in no way to be interpreted as the official policy of any Public Examining Body.

In examinations set by most CSE Boards, and at the Basic Level of the new GCSE examination as it is at present envisaged, the examiner is rarely, if at all, required to intervene whilst the pupil is speaking. In most role-plays at O and Alternative O Levels such interventions are usually the norm, and they will continue to be so in various forms at the Extended Level of the GCSE examination. Suggestions for the possible extension and development of each situation on this 'extended' basis are therefore included. These are only suggested developments and in no way should they be interpreted as prescriptive, since role-play is by definition an open-ended exercise in which the pupil is expected to take the initiative to a large degree. The possible lines along which role-play situations can be developed from the given rubric are obviously extensive and unpredictable.

In the actual examination, candidates do not see the examiner's instructions. For practice purposes however, there is much benefit to be gained from letting pupils have access to these so that they can have some idea as to the lines along which the situations may be developed. More able pupils might well assume the role of the examiner from time to time so that the situations can be worked out in pairs.

Emphasis on the use of such a preparation technique should not however detract from the fact that apart from actually visiting a German-speaking country, role-playing is the nearest the pupils come to practising the language in a real, life-related context. And herein lies its essential value. It is communicative, and in many respects a rehearsal for the real-life situations which pupils might well encounter in the country itself. Yet since practice in examination techniques will be perhaps the immediate and prime concern of pupils and teachers alike, the authors have given this aspect due emphasis in the book.

We hope it will prove a helpful and practical guide to all those who use it.

Introduction

Why?

If role-playing appears to be increasing in popularity as far as its inclusion in course-books and examinations is concerned, this is because the learning of foreign languages is increasingly being seen primarily as a means of communication, and the kind of language that is being taught is by and large that which you are most likely to need when visiting the foreign country whose language you are learning.

In other words, it is essentially a matter of rehearsal: of practising for situations which you may very well find yourself having to cope with at some time in the future. Moreover, since when you are abroad you are more likely to be asking questions than answering them, role-play does tend to lay more emphasis on the asking of questions, and the inclusion of role-play in examinations has revealed that this is an area in which traditionally not enough practice has been given.

How to set about it

Let's start by reminding you of some of the basic ways in which you can ask questions and ask for something.

You can, for instance, simply turn a statement round to formulate a question. So the statements ,,Du hast drei Geschwister'' and ,,Sie sind Engländer'' become as questions: ,,Hast du drei Geschwister?'' and ,,Sind Sie Engländer?'' Listen carefully to the way in which your teacher pronounces these two sentences, first as statements, and then as questions.

This is perhaps the most common way of asking a question in German. You can, of course, also use many question words like ,,Wo?'', ,,Wann?'', ,,Warum?'', ,,Wie?'', etc., and we will look at these in detail further on in the introduction. However if you're in a shop and you want to ask *for* something or you need to find out certain pieces of information, you can use other approaches.

Let's imagine, for example, that you are in a baker's shop and you want to buy some rolls. You should always start by greeting the shop assistant or by replying in an appropriate way to his or her greeting. For example, these greetings could be ,,Guten Morgen" or ,,Guten Tag". In some parts of Southern Germany as well as in Austria and Switzerland the greeting ,,Grüß Gott" is most commonly heard. Once you have exchanged greetings, you have three main ways of asking for what you want. Let's assume you want three rolls. You could say to the assistant:

,,Drei Brötchen, bitte."

Don't forget to include 'bitte'. It sounds very impolite if you don't.

Alternatively, you could say:

,,Ich hätte gern drei Brötchen, bitte."

And finally, a common way of asking for things in shops is to use the expression ,,Ich möchte . . ." meaning literally 'I would like . . .'. So in this case you would say:

,,Ich möchte bitte drei Brötchen."

Now it's your turn

Imagine that you're in a florist's. You want to buy five carnations. Give three different ways of asking for these, based on the examples above. (The word for carnation is 'die Nelke'; the plural form is 'Nelken'.)

A very common situation in which you might well find yourself is asking information from a passer-by in the street or seeking information from, let's say, a local tourist office. You can approach the situation in a variety of ways.

For example, if you stop a stranger in the street to ask him or her how to get to the railway station, you should always begin the conversation with a suitable greeting. You could say ,,Guten Tag. Entschuldigen Sie." The latter means literally 'Excuse me' and it is commonly used in German-speaking countries when addressing someone you don't know in the street. When the passer-by has replied, you could continue by asking:

,,Könnten Sie mir bitte helfen?"

Note that 'bitte' is included here as well.

You could then go on to ask your main question in three basic ways. Firstly you could ask:

„Könnten Sie mir bitte sagen, wo der Bahnhof ist?"

Alternatively you could phrase your question:

„Wie komme ich am besten zum Bahnhof?"

or

„Wo ist hier der Bahnhof, bitte?"

When you've found out what you want to know, you should always thank the person who has helped you by saying „Danke schön" or „Vielen Dank". And of course, before he or she leaves you you'll always say „Auf Wiedersehen."

Now it's your turn

Imagine you're on a street in a German town that you're visiting for the first time. You want to know where the post office is, and you stop a passer-by to ask him. Based on the examples above, give three ways of doing this. Don't forget to start the conversation in an appropriate way, and don't forget to thank the person when you've found out what you want to know. And of course the very last thing you'll say is „Auf Wiedersehen."

The word for post office is 'das Postamt'.

What do I have to do?

Whatever situation you find yourself in, you'll normally be required to perform one or more of the tasks we have listed here:

1 asking for information
2 giving an explanation
3 asking someone for something
4 paying for something
5 thanking somebody
6 apologising to somebody
7 complaining about something
8 describing something or somebody
9 choosing something

10 telephoning somebody
11 expressing your opinion about something
12 asking someone if they object to something

As we have already pointed out, you will be expected to go through the usual exchanges of greeting and farewell. You will soon find that although you are required to deal with a wide variety of situations, the actual number of questions you have to use is comparatively small. You should make sure that you are familiar with all these. You should then have no problem in dealing with the different situations in this book.

Now let's take a detailed look at each of the above categories or functions in turn.

1 Asking for information

Here are some of the most common questions, words and phrases you will need when asking for information. In each case we have given an example of how the item is used in context.

Gibt es ... ?
Gibt es ein Museum in dieser Stadt?

Wo ist hier ... ?
Wo ist hier ein Parkplatz, bitte?

Wohin?
Wohin fährt dieser Bus?

Haben⎱
Hätten⎰ *Sie vielleicht ... ?*

Hätten Sie vielleicht einen Stadtplan?

Könnten Sie mir bitte sagen, ... ?
Könnten Sie mir bitte sagen, ob hier in der Nähe ein Restaurant ist?

Wie ... ?
Wie ist Ihr Hotel?

Wie komme ich am besten ... ?
Wie komme ich am besten zum Bahnhof, bitte?

Was . . . ?
Was gibt es hier zu tun?

Wie lange . . . ?
Wie lange wohnen Sie schon in dieser Stadt?
(NB 'schon' is invariably used in this construction. It literally means 'already'. Note also that German uses the present tense here.)

Wann . . . ?
Wann beginnt der Film?

Seit wann . . . ?
Seit wann wohnen Sie hier?
(Note that the present tense is also used in this construction.)

Um wieviel Uhr . . . ?
Um wieviel Uhr fährt der letzte Bus?

Wie weit . . . ?
Wie weit ist es bis zum Bahnhof?

Wieviel(e) . . . ?
Wieviel kostet das?
Wieviele Einwohner hat Hamburg?

Welch(er/e/es/en/em) . . . ?
Welche Äpfel sind die billigsten?
In welchem Hotel wohnen Sie?

Was für . . . ?
Was für ein Auto haben Sie?

Wer . . . ?/Wen . . . ?/Wem . . . ?
Wer ist das?
Wen hast du heute in der Stadt gesehen?
Wem willst du das schenken?

Wessen . . . ?
Wessen Auto ist das?

Warum . . . ?
Warum bist du so spät aufgestanden?

möglich
Ist es möglich, das Frühstück im Zimmer einzunehmen?

Now it's your turn

Try using each of the items given above in a different situation from the one illustrated, e.g.

„Gibt es hier ein Hotel?"
„Wo ist hier das Rathaus?"

2   Explaining something

Here are some of the most common words and phrases you are likely to need when explaining something to other people. We have given examples of how each item can be used.

sein
Ich bin Engländer.
Sie ist Engländerin.

haben
Ich habe zwei Koffer im Taxi.

können
Ich kann leider heute nicht kommen.

weil ...
Ich kann leider nicht ins Kino gehen, weil ich nicht genug Geld habe.

müssen
Ich muß morgen früh abfahren.

wollen
Ich will morgen nachmittag ins Kino gehen.

brauchen
Ich brauche einen neuen Reifen.

verlieren
Ich habe meinen Reisepaß verloren.

verstehen
Ich habe leider nicht verstanden, was Sie eben gesagt haben.

spät; Verspätung
Ich bin zu spät aufgestanden.

Es war zu spät, Theaterkarten zu bekommen.
Der Zug hatte 12 Minuten Verspätung.

erst
Ich habe ihn erst heute gesehen.
Ich bin erst gestern angekommen.

gefallen
Das blaue Kleid gefällt mir gar nicht.

mögen
Das blaue Kleid mag ich nicht.

gern/lieber haben; tun, usw.
Ich trinke Kaffee gern.
Ich trinke lieber Bier.
Mir wäre eine Tasse Tee lieber.
Das tue ich gar nicht gern.

Now it's your turn

Try using each of the items given above in a different situation
from the one illustrated, e.g.

,,Er ist Engländer.''
,,Er hat einen Koffer im Auto.''

3   Asking someone for something

Here are some of the most common words, questions and
phrases you are likely to need when asking someone for
something. We have given examples of how each item can be
used.

Möchte
Ich möchte ein Einzelzimmer für eine Nacht.

hätte gern
Ich hätte gern zwei Birnen und vier Äpfel.

Könnten Sie mir bitte sagen ...?
Könnten Sie mir bitte sagen, wo die Bachstraße ist?

brauchen
Ich brauche einen neuen Reifen.

fehlen
Herr Ober! Es fehlt mir ein Messer.

Imperative
The Imperative Mood could be useful in this function, e.g.

Sprechen Sie bitte etwas lauter!

Now it's your turn

Try using each of the items given above in a different situation
from the one illustrated, e.g.

,,Ich möchte ein Doppelzimmer für vier Nächte.''

4 Paying for something

Here are some of the most common words, questions and
phrases you are likely to need when paying for something. We
have given examples of how each item can be used.

Wieviel . . . ?
Wieviel macht das?

kosten
Was kostet die Karte?
Wieviel kostet eine Rückfahrkarte nach Bamberg?

bekommen
Wieviel bekommen Sie von mir?

schuldig
Wieviel bin ich Ihnen noch schuldig?

Kleingeld
Haben Sie Kleingeld?

kleiner
Haben Sie es nicht kleiner?

geben
Ich gebe Ihnen DM 3,00.

teuer
Der Schlips ist aber sehr teuer!

billig
Das Buch ist billig.

Now it's your turn

Try using each of the items given above in a different situation
from the one illustrated, e.g.

„Wieviel kostet die Eintrittskarte?"
„Was kostet das Buch?"

5 Thanking somebody

Here are some of the most common words and phrases you are
likely to need when you are thanking somebody. We have given
examples of how each item can be used.

Danke
Danke schön!
Danke sehr!
Vielen Dank!
Recht herzlichen Dank!

danken
Ich danke Ihnen recht herzlich für die Einladung.

dankbar
Ich bin Ihnen sehr dankbar.

freundlich
Das ist aber sehr freundlich von Ihnen!

liebenswürdig
Das ist sehr liebenswürdig von Ihnen!

Now it's your turn

Try using each of the items given above in a different situation
from the one illustrated, e.g.

„Vielen Dank für das schöne Geschenk."
„Ich danke Ihnen für die schöne Geburtstagskarte."

6 Apologising to somebody

Here are some of the most common words and phrases you are
likely to need when you are apologising to somebody. We have
given examples of how each item can be used.

Verzeihung!
Verzeihung! Ich habe Sie nicht gesehen.

entschuldigen
Bitte, entschuldigen Sie!

leid tun
Das tut mir aber leid.
Es tut mir leid, daß ich dir nicht helfen kann.

bedauern
Ich bedauere, daß ich ihn nicht sehen konnte.

Now it's your turn

Try using each of the items given above in a different situation
from the one illustrated, e.g.

„Es tut mir leid, daß ich nicht kommen konnte."

7 Complaining about something

Here are some of the most common words and phrases you are
likely to need when you are complaining about something. We
have given examples of how each item can be used.

gefallen
Das Zimmer gefällt mir gar nicht.

zufrieden sein
Ich bin mit diesem Zimmer nicht zufrieden. Es ist zu klein.

sich beklagen
Ich muß mich über den Lärm beklagen.

sich ärgern
Ich ärgere mich darüber, daß Sie nicht früher angerufen haben.

erklären
Könnten Sie mir bitte erklären, warum mein Zimmer immer noch in Unordnung ist?

etwas gern (nicht gern) haben
Dieses Hotel habe ich nicht gern.

warten lassen
Sie haben mich eine halbe Stunde warten lassen.

Now it's your turn

Try using each of the items given above in a different situation from the one illustrated, e.g.

„Diese Schube gefallen mir nicht."

8 Describing something or somebody

Here are some of the most common words, questions and phrases you are likely to need when you are describing something or somebody. We have given examples of how certain items can be used.

Colour
Welche Farbe hat die Bluse?
braun; weiß; schwarz; gelb; blau;
hellbraun; hellblau; hellgrün;
dunkelbraun; dunkelblau; dunkelgrün;
bunt.
Das ist eine blaue Bluse.
Das ist ein brauner Anzug.
Das ist ein weißes Hemd.

Shape
rund; viereckig; oval.

Size
klein; ziemlich klein; relativ klein; sehr klein; zu klein.

groß; ziemlich groß; usw.
enorm; winzig; lang; kurz; breit; eng.

Material
aus Leder; aus Wolle; aus Baumwolle; aus Holz; aus Nylon; aus
Seide.

Pattern
einfarbig; gestreift; kariert; mit Tupfen.

Physical description
groß; klein; dick; dünn; alt; jung.
blond; dunkelhaarig; mit langen Haaren; kahlköpfig; eine Glatze
haben.

Personal characteristics
freundlich; Humor haben; ernst; zugänglich; aufgeschlossen;
höflich; nett; angenehm; vernünftig; ausgeglichen.
schweigsam; zurückhaltend; schüchtern; verschlossen; launisch;
unhöflich; unangenehm; unvernünftig; taktlos.

Now it's your turn

Try and use some of the words and phrases given above to
describe people you know and objects around you.

9 Choosing something

Here are some of the most common words and phrases you are
likely to need when choosing something. We have given
examples of how each item can be used.

nehmen
Ich nehme die gelbe Jacke.

lieber haben/etwas lieber tun
Ich habe den weißen Rock lieber.
Ich gehe lieber zu Fuß.

vorziehen
Ich ziehe den blauen Rock vor.
Ich ziehe es vor, zu Hause zu bleiben.

besser gefallen
Der blaue Rock gefällt mir besser.

brauchen
Er braucht einen Hammer.

geben
Geben Sie mir bitte drei Briefmarken zu DM 1,00!

Now it's your turn

Try using each of the items given above in a different situation
from the one illustrated, e.g.

,,Ich nehme die zwei Krawatten.''

10 Speaking to somebody on the telephone

Here are some of the most common words, questions and
phrases you are likely to need when you are speaking to
somebody on the telephone. We have given examples of how to
use the items in context.

Answering the telephone
Hallo. Hier ist John Smith.
Hallo. Wer ist am Apparat?
Hallo. Wer spricht?

On the telephone
Bleiben Sie bitte am Apparat!
Legen Sie bitte nicht auf!
Kann ich bitte mit Helga sprechen?
Ist Helga zu sprechen?
Kann ich etwas für Sie ausrichten?
Welche Nummer haben Sie?

Finishing a telephone conversation
Vielen Dank. Auf Wiederhören!

Now it's your turn

Try out some of the expressions given above by holding a short,
imaginary telephone conversation with one of your friends.

11 Expressing your opinion about something

Here are some of the most common words and phrases you are likely to need when you want to express your opinion about something. We have given examples of how each item can be used.

denken
Ich denke, daß der Rock viel zu teuer ist.

glauben
Ich glaube, daß er jetzt in Hameln wohnt.

halten für
Ich halte es für möglich.

der Meinung (der Ansicht) sein
Ich bin der Meinung, daß er heute noch kommt.

meiner Meinung nach
Meiner Meinung nach war der Film langweilig.

dagegen
Ich will das nicht tun. Ich bin dagegen.

übereinstimmen
Ich stimme mit dir überein.

egal
Das ist mir völlig egal.

schon
This word is useful with verbs like 'glauben' when you want to show you agree with the question that has been put to you, e.g.

,,Wird es heute noch regnen?''
,,Ich glaube schon.''

Now it's your turn

Try using each of the items given above in a different situation from the one illustrated.

,,Ich denke, daß der Film wirklich spannend war.''

12 Asking someone if he or she objects to something

Here are some of the most common words, questions and phrases you are likely to need when you are asking someone if he or she objects to something. We have given examples of how each item can be used.

stören
Stört Sie mein Radio?
Störe ich Sie bei der Arbeit?
Stört es Sie, wenn ich rauche?

ausmachen
Macht Ihnen das etwas aus?

dagegen
Ich möchte rauchen. Haben Sie etwas dagegen?
Haben Sie etwas dagegen, wenn ich rauche?

Now it's your turn

Try using each of the items given above in a different situation from the one illustrated, e.g.

,,Stört es dich, wenn ich meine Schallplatten spiele?''

Preparing a role-play situation

Vocabulary

The vocabulary that you will need in role-playing is the basic vocabulary that you have been learning throughout your course. As you prepare the situations in this book, make sure that you revise all the common items that you might want to buy in shops, the food and drink you might wish to order in a restaurant and the information you might require at a travel agency or a tourist information bureau. If you come across a particular word or phrase you don't know, then try and find a way of expressing the same idea by using different words.

Playing a part

You must also bear in mind that in the role-playing situations you will be playing a particular part, and although, obviously, you don't have to be a great actor or actress, you will need to work out the exact details of the role assigned to you. Try to imagine that you really are in Germany, Austria or Switzerland, in the situation you have been given, and ask yourself, 'Using the German I know, how can I get this idea across?'

Relationship

The first thing you must do is to establish what your exact relationship is with the person or persons to whom you are speaking. If you are speaking to someone you do not know well and who is older than you are, then the relationship will be a formal one. In this instance you must remember to use the 'Sie' form of address. If the other person is a friend, a young person of about your own age or younger, or a member of your 'host' family, you must use the 'du' form. Remember that if you are talking to more than one person in the familiar form, you must use 'ihr'. (If this type of situation arose in an examination, you would lose marks for not using the correct form of address or for using it inconsistently.)

Studying the background information

You must always make sure that you are fully aware of all the details of the situation you are required to play. If you are told, for example, that you are in a restaurant with only DM 20 in your pocket, don't spend more money than you actually have. Similarly, if you are told that you have been waiting for a bus for a long time, don't say that you left home three minutes previously . . . Always be consistent within the terms of the role.

Conveying the Message

The most important thing to bear in mind about all the points that you have to get across in order to convey the message, is that you are not being asked to *translate* word for word from English into German. In fact in an examination, the instructions are usually phrased in such a way that if you do try to translate them word for word you will soon get into enormous difficulties. You must get the *basic idea* across. You will never be asked to say something that you haven't already prepared for during your course. As we suggested before, try and find a way of expressing the ideas in words with which you are familiar.

There are often several different ways in which you can get the same idea across. For example, if you are told to suggest to a friend that you should go and have a coffee, you could say:

,,Wie wäre es mit einer Tasse Kaffee?''

or

,,Hättest du Zeit, mit mir Kaffee zu trinken?''

or

,,Möchtest du vielleicht eine Tasse Kaffee mit mir trinken?''

You might be told to ask the price of a dress in a shop. Here you could say:

,,Was kostet das Kleid?''

or

,,Wieviel kostet das Kleid?''

Now it's your turn

Find different ways of:

1 suggesting that you and a friend go to the cinema
2 asking the price of a green shirt.

Developing the situation

If you actually found yourself in one of the situations in a German-speaking country, then it is most likely that something unexpected might happen. For example, you might find that the greengrocer has sold out of tomatoes, and that he asks you if you would like something else instead. In an examination, you might encounter the same sort of thing, with the examiner intervening in such a way that you have to say something which makes the situation develop. You should always try to think about the possible variations and extensions of the situation before you start playing your role, and not allow yourself to be taken unawares.

You must always listen very carefully to what the other person is saying and adapt your own role and what you say accordingly. Don't forget that the other person's intervention is giving you a further opportunity of expressing yourself in German, and always try to take the initiative and say as much as you can. Never restrict yourself to one-word answers, or simply reply with 'Ja' or 'Nein'.

In an examination, the examiner will have instructions as to how he or she might try to extend and develop the situation – if, of course, the candidate lets him or her do this. If the candidate ignores what the examiner says and simply goes on abruptly to the next point in the role, then marks will be lost.

In the practice situations in this book we have included the kind of instructions the examiner might well have been given for that particular situation. On occasions your teacher may want you to look at these instructions, or on others you might be asked to cover them up so that you have to think out the development of the role yourself. If you are preparing for the role-plays of certain Examining Bodies, you will not always have to cope with interventions. Nevertheless, it is still good practice for you, as you will doubtless encounter such interventions when you visit a German-speaking country.

Overacting

Talking is not the same thing as acting. Although you are playing a part, you should never feel that you have to act as though you were on the stage. Don't gesture and don't shout. Remember that all you have to do is to get your points across, to find out the required information and adapt your role to the interventions of the other person and the needs of the situation. You are, after all, in an examination gaining marks for the quality of the language you are using, not your acting ability.

Examples of situations

Here are three situations, with an example of how the conversation might possibly go. Obviously, as in real life, someone else might have a totally different conversation based on the same instructions.

Example situation 1

You are in a train, and speak to the person sitting opposite you.

1 Ask if he minds if you open the window.

2 Ask if he/she is going far.

3 Ask if there is a restaurant car on the train.

4 Invite him/her to go with you for a meal.

Fellow passenger

1 Say you don't mind, but it is snowing outside. Wouldn't it be better just to turn down the heating?

2 Say you are going to Frankfurt. Where is he/she going?

   Does he/she live there? It's a long journey, isn't it? Has he/she already eaten?

3 There is, in the middle of the train.

4 Accept invitation.

How it works

A Macht es Ihnen etwas aus, wenn ich das Fenster öffne?

B Nein, das macht mir nichts aus, aber es schneit doch. Wäre es nicht besser, die Heizung auf klein zu stellen?

A Ich möchte lieber etwas frische Luft. Fahren Sie eigentlich weit?

B Ich fahre nach Frankfurt. Und Sie, wohin fahren Sie?

A Ich fahre nach München.

B Wohnen Sie dort?

A Nein, ich fahre geschäftlich.

B Das ist aber eine lange Reise. Haben Sie schon gegessen?

A Nein, noch nicht. Ich habe aber Hunger. Wissen Sie, ob dieser Zug einen Speisewagen hat?

B Ja, in der Mitte des Zuges.

A Nun, Sie sind doch sicher auch hungrig. Wollen Sie mit mir essen gehen?

B Gerne. Eine ausgezeichnete Idee. Gehen wir.

Example situation 2

You are at home, and telephone a German friend, Manfred. Manfred's brother answers the phone, and tells you that Manfred is out.

1 Ask when he will be back.

2 Ask if he received your letter this morning.

3 Ask if he has decided to go out with you this evening.

4 Say you have tickets for a concert and ask if Manfred will ring you when he comes in.

Manfred's brother

1 Say he has gone to the library, and you don't know when he will be back. Can you take a message?

2 Say you don't think he got a letter today. When was it posted?

3 Say you know he intends to go out this evening, but you don't know who with. Where is he/she thinking of going?

4 Ask for his/her telephone number and if he/she will be at home all afternoon.

How it works

A Wann wird er wieder zu Hause sein?

B Er ist in die Bibliothek gegangen, und ich weiß nicht, wann er zurückkommen wird. Kann ich ihm etwas ausrichten?

A Ja, bitte. Wissen Sie, ob er heute morgen meinen Brief bekommen hat?

B Ich glaube nicht. Wann haben Sie ihn aufgegeben?

A Gestern abend, gegen zehn Uhr.

B Dann wird er wahrscheinlich heute nachmittag ankommen.

A Schön. Ich wollte gern wissen, ob er heute abend mit mir ausgehen will.

B Ich weiß, daß er vorhat, auszugehen, aber ich weiß nicht, mit wem. Wohin wollen Sie gehen?

A Ich habe zwei Konzertkarten, und ich möchte, daß Manfred mit mir geht. Könnten Sie ihn bitten, mich anzurufen, wenn er zurückkommt?

B Gerne. Welche Nummer haben Sie?

A Meine Nummer ist 47 22 63.

B 47 22 63. Gut. Sind Sie heute nachmittag die ganze Zeit zu Hause?

A Ja, ich werde auf seinen Anruf warten.

B Ich werde es ihm ausrichten.

A Vielen Dank und Auf Wiederhören!

B Auf Wiederhören!

Shopping

Situation 1

You go into a _Bäckerei_, and speak to the shop assistant.

1 Ask for two loaves of bread.

2 Ask for eight rolls.

3 Say you would like a cake; ask which he/she recommends.

4 Ask how much you owe, and pay.

Vocabulary

das Brot (Weißbrot/Schwarzbrot)
das Brötchen
empfehlen
Wieviel macht das?
der Streuselkuchen (= _flat yeast cake_)
der Napfkuchen (= _cake baked in a special mould_)
der Nußstollen

Shop assistant

1   Ask what kind of loaves.

2   Say you have only four left. Does he/she want to wait?

3   Suggest *Streuselkuchen* or *Napfkuchen*.

    Would he/she like a loaf with nut filling?

4   Cost is between DM 8,00 and DM 30,00 depending on purchases.

Situation 2

You go into a *Konditorei*, and speak to the shopkeeper.

1 Ask for a Black Forest gateau and six doughnuts.

2 Say you want Danish pastries.

3 Ask how much the cream meringues in the window are, and buy four.

4 Ask how much it all comes to, and offer a 50-Mark note.

Vocabulary

die Schwarzwälder Kirschtorte
der Berliner (Pfannkuchen)
die Schnecke
das Sahnebaiser
der Fünfzigmarkschein
eine halbe Stunde
das Kleingeld

Shopkeeper

1 Say that you have just sold the last doughnut, but there will be more in half an hour.

2 You have only two left, but there are some very nice small cakes.

3 Say the cream meringues are DM 1,80 each.

4 Say how much it costs and ask if he/she has any change. (Cost is DM 25,50.)

Situation 3

You are out shopping and you go into a *Delikatessengeschäft*. You speak to the shopkeeper.

1 Ask how much the ham costs, and when he/she has told you, buy half a kilo.

2 Ask which sausage he/she recommends, and buy 250 grams.

3 Order a roast chicken for tomorrow.

4 Apologise for only having a 50-Mark note.

Vocabulary

der Schinken
ein halbes Kilo
die Wurst
das Brathähnchen
für morgen

Shopkeeper

1   Say you have some at DM 22,00 a kilo, but the more
    expensive one is better. When asked, say it is DM 26,00 a
    kilo.

2   Offer various types of sausage: *Schinkenwurst, Mettwurst,
    Salami,* etc. Recommend the *Blutwurst* that you have just
    made, at DM 14,00 a kilo.

3   What weight of chicken? (From 2 to 4 kilos.) When will he/she
    come to collect it?

4   Say the bill (without chicken) comes to either DM 14,50 or
    DM 19,00.

Situation 4

You are in a clothes shop in Germany. You have seen a dress (or a shirt) in the shop window, but you cannot see it in the shop. You have a maximum of DM 140,00 to spend. You speak to a sales assistant.

1 Ask about the dress (or the shirt).

2 Ask if you can try it on.

3 Ask if he/she has any belts (or ties) to go with it.

4 Say you prefer one of the belts (or ties) and ask how much it is.

Vocabulary

das Kleid
das Hemd
anprobieren
der Gürtel
die Krawatte
aus Leder
aus Kunststoff

Sales assistant

1 Ask for exact details of the dress (or shirt).

2 Say it costs DM 120,00.

Would he/she like to try on something else as well? Ask his/her opinion of other items.

3 What kind of belt (leather, synthetic, wide/narrow, colour, etc.) or tie (material, colour, stripes, etc.).

4 It is DM 12,00, but you have a better one for DM 25,00.

Ask if he/she wishes to buy.

Situation 5

You go into a clothes shop. You have just bought a new jacket and want to buy matching garments. You speak to the sales assistant.

1 Say you want to buy a shirt (or blouse) to match your new jacket, and buy one of those offered.

2 Say you also need a tie (or jumper), and choose one of those offered.

3 Ask if they have any nylon socks (or woollen gloves), and buy two pairs.

4 Ask if they accept cheques or credit cards.

Vocabulary

das Hemd
die Bluse
die Jacke
passen zu (= *match*)
der Pullover
zwei Paar $\begin{cases} \text{Nylonsocken} \\ \text{Wollhandschuhe} \end{cases}$
der Scheck
die Kreditkarte

Sales assistant

1 Ask the colour and what the jacket is made of, and offer two
shirts/blouses, one at DM 40,00, one at DM 60,00.

2 Offer choice of ties at DM 18,00 each or jumpers at DM 50,00
or DM 70,00.

3 Ask what colour socks or gloves and whether plain or
patterned. Offer them at DM 6,00 a pair (socks) and DM 10,00
a pair (gloves).

4 Present bill and accept cheque or credit card. Bill will vary
from DM 64,00 to DM 140,00 depending on items chosen.

Situation 6

You are a German man/woman, Herr/Frau Schmidt. You are in a German market, and you go to the stall of a greengrocer you know quite well.

1 Ask how he/she is, and ask about his/her family.

2 Say you want some large onions.

3 Ask for a cauliflower and a cabbage.

4 Buy a kilo of pears.

Vocabulary

die Familie
die Zwiebel
der Blumenkohl
der Kohl
die Birne
das Obst

Greengrocer

1 Ask how he/she likes his/her new job. Does he/she have to travel a lot?

2 Are these onions large enough? Recommend some cheaper ones.

3 Offer various sizes and prices. Say the cabbages are not very fresh, but you are expecting some more later on.

Ask if he/she would like some fruit today.

4 Tell him/her the price: about DM 12,00 to DM 15,00, depending on what he/she has bought.

Situation 7

You are in a supermarket and see a man drop a purse. You try to catch him but he goes out of the shop before you can do so. You look inside the purse and then go to see the manager.

1 Say you saw the man drop the purse.

2 Say that you have opened the purse but there is no name or address in it.

3 Describe the contents of the purse.

Ask what the manager will do if the man doesn't collect the purse.

Vocabulary

das Portemonnaie
fallen lassen
der Name
die Adresse
abholen
zurückgeben

Manager

1   Ask why he/she didn't give it back to the man.

2   Ask what the man was like.

    Ask what is in the purse.

3   Say you will give it to the police, but ask for his/her name
    and address.

Situation 8

You are visiting some friends for lunch and you want to buy some flowers for your host and hostess. You go to a florist's shop. You do not want to spend more than DM 10,00.

1 Say you want to buy some flowers.

2 Ask the florist for some advice.

3 Find out the prices and choose some flowers.

4 Buy the flowers, then ask the way to the nearest underground station.

Vocabulary

Rat geben

fünf Stück $\begin{cases} \text{Rosen} \\ \text{Tulpen} \end{cases}$

die Farbe
die U-Bahnstation
die Bushaltestelle

Florist

1   Is it for a present? For someone special?

2   Suggest roses or tulips.

3   Large roses are DM 12,00 for five, smaller ones DM 9,00;
    tulips are DM 6,00 for five.

    Ask which colour.

4   It is quite a long way, but there is a bus stop opposite. Where
    is he/she going?

    The number 10 bus stops near there.

Situation 9

You have arranged to meet a friend outside a big department store in a German town. You arrive early, so you decide to look around the shop. You go to the information desk and speak to the shop assistant.

1 Ask where the toy department is.

2 Ask if you can get there in the lift.

3 Ask if there is a café in the shop and if lunch is served there.

4 Ask at what time the shop usually shuts and if there is an evening when it stays open late.

Vocabulary

die Spielwarenabteilung
im vierten Stock
der Fahrstuhl
außer Betrieb
die Rolltreppe
die Imbißstube

Shop assistant

1 Say that it is on the fourth floor and that there is an excellent choice. What is he/she looking for?

2 Yes, but the lift is out of order. Suggest escalator or stairs.

3 The main café is on the top floor; lunch will be over now, but there is a snack bar on the first floor. Will that do? What does he/she want to eat?

4 The shop usually shuts at 6 p.m. and there is no late evening shopping. Does he/she know the supermarket in the same street? It stays open until 9 p.m. several evenings a week.

Situation 10

You are staying in a German town and you are out shopping.
Soon after coming out of a large store you realise that you no
longer have your wallet/handbag. You go back into the shop and
ask to speak to the manager/manageress.

1 Apologise for bothering him/her.

2 Tell him/her about losing your wallet/handbag.

3 Ask what you should do.

4 Ask if he/she thinks there is a chance that it might be found.

Vocabulary

die Störung
die Brieftasche
die Handtasche
der Verkäufer
die Verkäuferin
die Polizeiwache

Manager/manageress

1 Say it doesn't matter and ask how you can help.

2 Exactly when and where was the handbag/wallet lost? Which assistant was helping him/her at the time? Has he/she spoken to the assistant about the loss?

Ask what was in the wallet/handbag.

3 Suggest that he/she reports it to the nearest police station. Does he/she know where that is? Give directions.

4 Yes, there is a chance someone might return it to your office, but there are a lot of thieves about. Does he/she think it might have been stolen, or did he/she drop it?

Suggest that he/she comes back the next day.

Situation 11

You go into a grocer's shop, and speak to the grocer.

1 Ask for 100 grams of ham and a tin of sardines.

2 Say you would like some cheese.

3 Ask him/her to recommend some good wine. Buy two bottles and also a bottle of apple juice.

4 Choose a packet of biscuits and a bar of chocolate.

Vocabulary

eine Dose Sardinen
die Flasche
der Apfelsaft
das Paket Kekse
eine Tafel Schokolade
dick/dünn geschnitten

Grocer

1 Thick slices of ham or thin? Portuguese or French sardines?

2 Ask what kind of cheese he/she prefers (hard, soft, cream, blue, etc.).

3 What is the wine to go with? Make appropriate suggestions. Wine costs DM 1,90, DM 3,50, and DM 7,80.

   Recommend various kinds of biscuits and chocolate.

4 Is that everything? Ask for payment.

Situation 12

You go into a greengrocer's shop in Germany, but you do not have much money, so you must buy the cheapest fruit and vegetables. You speak to the greengrocer.

1   Buy one cauliflower and a kilo of onions.

2   Ask for the greengrocer's advice on other vegetables.

3   Ask about peaches and pears and decide which fruit to buy.

4   Ask for half a kilo of tomatoes.

Vocabulary

das Gemüse
der Pfirsich
die Tomate
die Bohne
der Champignon

Greengrocer

1. Large or small cauliflower? Large are DM 5,00, small are DM 3,50. Onions are DM 3,00.

2 Beans are good value at DM 4,00 a kilo, and mushrooms at DM 4,80.

3 Peaches are DM 6,00 a kilo, pears DM 5,00 a kilo. Suggest apples at DM 3,50 a kilo.

4 No tomatoes at present; they will arrive later. Would he/she like to come back?

   Ask if he/she would like something else. Ask for payment.

Situation 13

You go into a shop, and speak to the shop assistant.

1 Say you were in the shop earlier, and you think you left an umbrella behind.

2 Say it was blue and white and not very long.

3 Describe the assistant who served you.

4 Ask if the shop will get in touch with you if it is found.

Vocabulary

vergessen
der Regenschirm
verständigen
bedienen
die Telefonnummer

Shop assistant

1 Ask what time he/she was in the shop. What was the umbrella like?

2 Ask who it was who served him/her.

3 Ask if he/she remembers exactly where the umbrella was left.

4 Ask for name, address and telephone number.

Situation 14

You are staying in a German town and have been involved in a slight accident. A jacket (or a dress) that you want to wear this evening has been slightly torn and needs cleaning. You go to a dry cleaner's, and speak to an assistant.

1 Say you want the jacket/dress cleaned.

2 Find out when the garment will be ready.

3 Ask if it can be repaired as well.

4 Ask if it can be delivered to your hotel when it is ready.

Vocabulary

(chemisch) reinigen
fertig
reparieren
liefern
die Zusatzgebühr
der Fleck
der Riß
dringend

Assistant

1 Find out what the stains are and how the accident happened.

2 It will be ready in two days' time.

   It can only be ready today with extra payment, and even then it might not be ready. But let yourself be persuaded.

3 You do repairs, but clothes have to be sent away, so it won't be back for a few days. The tear is not very serious: suggest that he/she could repair it.

4 You do not normally deliver. Why is it so urgent?

   What time is it needed? Which hotel? As it is so near, you can deliver it when you leave work.

Situation 15

You go into a dry cleaner's in Germany, and speak to the assistant.

1 Ask to have your dress (or trousers) cleaned.

2 Ask when the garment will be ready as you will be leaving the next day.

3 Ask how much it will cost.

4 Ask if the dress/trousers can be delivered to your hotel as you will be out all day.

Vocabulary

ins Hotel liefern
normal
expreß
vor Geschäftsschluß

Assistant

1 Ask what has been spilt on it/them.

2 Explain that the ordinary service takes two days, but there is an express service that takes two hours.

3 The ordinary service is DM 6,00. The express service is DM 9,00. Which will he/she have?

4 Ask which hotel he/she is staying at.

Suggest he/she calls just before closing time (7 p.m.) or early next morning (shop opens at 8 a.m.).

At the restaurant

Situation 16

You are in a restaurant with a friend.

1 Ask your friend if he/she has decided what to eat.

2 Ask what kind of wine he/she would prefer.

3 Ask if he/she has been to this place before.

4 Ask what he/she would like to do later on.

Vocabulary

der Hauswein
der Flaschenwein
ziemlich teuer
das Kino
das Theater
das Konzert

Friend

1   Say you are not sure. What does he/she think?

2   Say you don't like what is suggested and suggest something
    else.

    Will the house wine do as the other wines are rather
    expensive?

3   Say you haven't been here before. Has he/she? If yes, was
    the food good? If not, how did he/she come to hear of it?

4   Would he/she like to go to the cinema? If yes, what kind of
    film does he/she prefer? If no, what about the theatre or a
    concert?

Situation 17

You go into a restaurant with a friend who does not speak German. You do not want to spend more than DM 24,00 each. You speak to the waiter.

1 Ask if there is a free table.

2 Ask for the menu and for the waiter's advice.

3 Say that that is too expensive and ask how much chicken and chips would cost.

4 Ask waiter to recommend wine.

Vocabulary

frei
die Speisekarte
der Kalbsbraten
das Brathähnchen
die Pommes frites (*pl.*)
die Vorspeise
das Hauptgericht

58

Waiter

1   Ask for how many people and where they would like to sit.

2   Recommend the roast veal. It costs DM 20,00 each.

3   Chicken and chips is DM 15,00.

Ask if they would like an hors d'œuvre before their main course.

4   Suggest a Riesling at DM 12,50 a bottle, or house wine at DM 6,00.

Ask if they would like an aperitif.

Situation 18

You are in a restaurant in Germany with a friend who does not speak German, so you must order for him/her as well as for yourself. You do not want to spend more than DM 60,00 in all.

1   Ask if there is a fixed-price menu.

2   Find out what choice is offered for the cheapest meal.

3   Ask if wine is included and order some.

4   Ask if you will have to wait long, as you are in a hurry.

Vocabulary

das Gedeck/Menü
das billigste Gericht
einschließlich
es eilig haben
eine Karaffe Wein
die Weinkarte

Waiter

1   There are two menus, one at DM 20,00 and one at DM 35,00.

2   There is a choice of *Brathähnchen, Beefsteak,* or
    Kalbsbraten.

    Ask which vegetables they would like.

3   Service is included, but not wine.

    Say the house wine is very good, and give them a wine list.

    Ask which hors d'œuvre they would like (*Suppe,
    Mayonnaiseei, Salatplatte*).

4   Say you will serve them straight away.

Situation 19

You are in a restaurant in Germany with a friend who does not speak German. Neither of you has enjoyed the meal and you send for the manager to express your dissatisfaction.

1 Complain about the meat not being properly cooked.

2 The service was poor; and you had to wait too long between courses.

3 The waiter forgot to bring the glass of water you had asked for.

4 There is a mistake in the bill.

Vocabulary

sich beschweren
die Bedienung
das Glas Wasser
die Rechnung
nicht stimmen

Manager

1 Find out what was ordered and what instructions given.

2 Explain that the waiter is new. Did they tell him they were in a hurry?

3 Apologise about water. Would they like a drink now?

4 Identify the error. Say the waiter is not used to their prices.

Apologise and change bill.

Promise better service in future.

Situation 20

You are on holiday in Germany, and you are the only one in your party who can speak German. You go into a restaurant and speak to the waiter/waitress.

1 Ask if they have a table free.

2 Try to get a table on the terrace overlooking the garden.

3 Order the fixed-price meal for everyone.

4 Order the drinks to go with the meal.

Vocabulary

die Terrasse
Es ist kühl
der Speisesaal
der Nachtisch

Waiter/waitress

1 Ask how many in party and where they would like to sit.

2 Say there is one table left on the terrace but it is rather cool outside. Would they prefer an inside table?

3 Say there are three fixed-price meals. Which one would they like?

Ask which starter, main course, vegetables, and dessert they would like.

At the hotel

Situation 21

You have just arrived at a hotel in Germany with your parents and your brother who do not speak German. You speak to the hotel receptionist.

1 Say you want two double rooms for one night.

2 Say you would like rooms which look onto the garden and that are near one another.

3 Ask the price of the rooms including breakfast.

4 Ask what time breakfast is served and if you can have it in the bedroom.

Vocabulary

das Doppelzimmer
auf den Garten gehen
der Zimmerpreis
im Erdgeschoß
abreisen
früh am Morgen

Receptionist

1 For how many people? With bath?

  Offer one on the ground floor and one on the second floor.

2 Say there are two together on the first floor, but only one looks onto the garden.

3 The rooms are DM 60,00 each. Breakfast is DM 10,00 extra.

4 Breakfast is 7.30 to 9.15 a.m. Will they be leaving early?

Situation 22

You are on holiday in Germany with your family, consisting of
father, mother, a 16-year-old girl, and her twin brother. You
may play the part of any member of the family you choose, but
you are the only one who speaks German. You go into a hotel
and speak to the receptionist.

1   Ask if you can have some rooms.

2   You would prefer rooms with a good view, and not too close
    to the kitchen.

3   Decide whether to accept what you are offered, and ask if
    you can have dinner in the hotel.

4   Ask if there is a lift and if you can have help with your
    luggage.

Vocabulary

die Aussicht
der Fahrstuhl
das Gepäck
der Träger

Receptionist

1 Ask what he/she requires. How many people/rooms? Other
   requirements (bath/shower)?

2 You have one room on the ground floor (not close to the
   kitchen), and two on the second floor.

3 Yes. What time would they like dinner? Would they like
   breakfast in their rooms the next morning? At what time?

4 There is a lift. The porter will help. Where is the luggage?

Situation 23

You are staying in a hotel in Germany and you are the only member of your family who can speak German. Your young brother has been ill during the night. The following morning you speak to the receptionist.

1 Explain the problem.

2 Ask about local doctors.

3 Ask about possibility of changing rooms because of traffic noise.

4 Ask about possibility of providing meals in bedroom.

Vocabulary

Es war ihm schlecht
Fieber haben
der `Arzt
das Zimmer wechseln
der Lärm
das Ärzteverzeichnis
die Sprechstunde

Receptionist

1 Express concern and enquire about illness (was it sudden, possible causes, etc.).

2 Suggest names of doctors. Is boy fit to go to surgery? If so, give times. If not, offer to ask doctor to visit.

3 Say the only room available is on the top floor. Will that do, or will they wait until the next day?

4 Usually only serve breakfast in bedrooms, but can take up lunch and dinner. For mother/father too? What would he/they like to eat?

On the telephone

Situation 24

You are at home and telephone a German friend who has been ill.

1 Ask what has been the matter and if he/she is better.

2 Ask if he/she is able to get up now.

3 Ask if there is anything you can do to help.

4 Ask if he/she would like some fruit – grapes or oranges.

Vocabulary

Was hat dir gefehlt?
sich besser fühlen
etwas tun
die Weintraube
sich nicht anstrengen
die Zeitschrift

Friend

1 Say you have had 'flu, but are feeling much better now.

Ask if he/she will come and see you as you can't go out for a few days.

2 You can get up, but you must take things easy.

3 Ask him/her to bring you a magazine that you like.

4 You don't feel much like eating fruit, but you would like something to drink.

Situation 25

You telephone a German friend.

1   Apologise for not having turned up to meet him/her yesterday.

2   Suggest meeting on Saturday.   *sich treffen*

3   Would he/she like to go with you to a party at a friend's house?

4   Arrange details of meeting.

Vocabulary

Es tut mir leid
gestern
die Party
Was war los?

74

Friend

1   Ask what happened.

Why didn't he/she telephone before?

2   Saturday is difficult. You have a lot to do. What is he/she thinking of doing?

3   Ask for details (when, where, dress, etc.).

4   Agree to go.

You might be able to borrow your parents' car. Would he/she like a lift?

Situation 26

You have been staying in a German town, but have not been well, and this has prevented you from getting in touch with a friend whom you had promised to contact. You now telephone him/her.

1 Apologise and explain why you have not been in touch.

2 Suggest a meeting: give time and place.

3 Suggest where you can go together.

4 You need to buy a good German dictionary, but you do not know where to go to buy it.

Vocabulary

sich treffen
das Wörterbuch
Das macht nichts
der Dom
zu Mittag essen

Friend

1 Accept apology and ask how he/she is now.

2 You would like to meet, but time and place not suitable.
Suggest alternative and make arrangements.

3 You need to buy a new coat; will he/she help you choose?

4 Suggest Merck or Langemann in the Schillerstraße. Say you
will take him/her there after having met at the cathedral.

Suggest having a meal together: time depending on
arrangements already made. Discuss kind of restaurant you
might go to.

Situation 27

You are staying in a German town and you telephone a German friend.

1 Suggest that you meet.

2 Invite him/her out to a meal.

3 Ask him/her to recommend a good restaurant.

4 Choose one of the places recommended and arrange meeting.

Vocabulary

einladen
sehr nett
keine Zeit haben
deutsche ⎫
italienische ⎬Küche
mit dem Wagen abholen

Friend

1 You would be delighted, but when and where?

2 Accept, but you are not free on day suggested. Suggest another day.

   Ask whether it is for lunch or dinner.

3 What kind of restaurant has he/she in mind (large, small, German, Italian)?

   Recommend several restaurants in the town centre.

4 Ask exactly where he/she is staying.

   Suggest either meeting at entrance to underground station, or collecting him/her in your car.

Situation 28

It is your birthday and you have received a present of a blouse (or a shirt) from a German friend. You telephone your friend.

1 Express your thanks.

2 Say what you are doing to celebrate your birthday.

3 Ask if you can go and stay with him/her during the summer holidays.

4 Ask about the health of other members of the family.

Vocabulary

der Geburtstag
feiern
die Sommerferien
Wie geht es . . .?
Alles Gute zum Geburtstag!
gefallen (Gefällt dir . . .?)
stehen (Steht dir . . .?)
fleißig arbeiten

Friend

1 Wish him/her a happy birthday.

 Ask if he/she likes the colour, and if the shirt/blouse suits him/her.

2 Ask what other presents he/she has had.

3 Ask when he/she wants to come and for how long. Explain your own holiday plans.

4 Say they are all well, but your sister is tired as she is working very hard for her exams. Ask about his/her family.

 Ask why he/she hasn't written recently.

Situation 29

You are in a German town on your way to stay with some friends. Unfortunately your plane was late arriving, and you have missed the last train to your friends' small town. You telephone your friends.

1 Ask if anyone has gone to meet you at the station yet.

2 Explain what has happened and apologise for being late.

3 Ask what you should do next.

4 Say you will catch a train the following morning.

Vocabulary

vom Bahnhof abholen
den Zug nehmen
eben dabei sein
der Flug
Verspätung haben
gegenüber

Friend

1 You were just about to get the car out of the garage. Where is he/she phoning from?

2 Ask why the flight was delayed.

3 When is the next train?

4 Has he/she enough money to stay in a hotel? If yes, try the large hotel opposite the station. If no, would he/she like you to come by car to pick him/her up?

Does he/she know times of trains the next morning?

Has he/she had a meal? If not, suggest he/she has something to eat.

Situation 30

You are telephoning a friend who lives in a German town.

1 Say you are coming to that town for a few days and would like to see him/her.

2 Ask how far your hotel on the outskirts of that town is from your friend's house.

3 Suggest that you visit a museum together.

4 Ask about getting to this meeting by bus or underground.

Vocabulary

auf ein paar Tage
das Museum
mit dem Bus
mit der U-Bahn
den ganzen Tag
Zeit haben

Friend

1 Say you would love to meet, but will be working all day, so which day will he/she be free in the evening?

Invite him/her to dinner one evening.

2 Offer to go and fetch him/her by car.

3 Ask what he/she would like to see most, and agree with suggestion of a museum.

4 If bus, suggest underground might be quicker and cheaper. If underground, suggest bus might be more interesting.

Ask time and place of meeting.

At the garage

Situation 31

You are in your parents' car in Germany, but your parents cannot speak German. You stop at a filling station, and speak to the petrol pump attendant.

1 Ask for some petrol, and ask him/her to check the oil and the tyre pressure.

2 Ask how far it is to the nearest town.

3 Ask if you can buy cigarettes and sweets.

4 Ask how much it comes to, and if you can pay by credit card.

Vocabulary

das Benzin
das Öl
der Reifendruck
überprüfen
die Kreditkarte
Super
Normal
ein halber Liter

Pump attendant

1 Ask what kind of petrol and how much.

 Tell him/her that it needs half a litre of oil, but the tyres don't need any air.

2 It is about 20 km, but if they are looking for somewhere to have lunch, there is a good restaurant in a village about 5 km away.

3 Say yes, and ask what he/she would like.

4 Work out price at DM 1,50 a litre for petrol, and DM 1,80 for oil, plus cigarettes and sweets.

Situation 32

You are on a motoring holiday in Germany, but are the only one in your party to speak German. You go to a filling station, and speak to a petrol pump attendant.

1 Buy petrol and get oil checked.

2 Ask where the toilet is.

3 Ask if one can buy sweets and drinks for the children.

4 Ask what there is to see and do in the nearest town.

Vocabulary

die Toilette
hinten
ein Getränk
die nächste Stadt
das Gebäude
die Kirche
das Schwimmbad
der Reitstall

Pump attendant

1 Ask how much petrol and what kind.

2 The toilet is at the back: first door on the left.

3 Say there are no hot drinks; what cold drinks would they like?

There are no sweets left; they will have to go to the nearest town for sweets.

4 What kind of places do they like to visit? Depending on answer, suggest: old buildings, churches, market-place, etc. What kind of activities do they prefer? Depending on answer, suggest: swimming-pool, park, horse-riding, etc.

Ask where they come from and how long they are staying.

If necessary, ask to be paid for petrol and drinks.

In the street

Situation 33

You have witnessed an accident, and you approach a policeman who has just arrived.

1 Say that it was you who telephoned the police.

2 Tell him that you saw what happened.

3 Say that you were standing at the bus stop when a little boy ran out into the road in front of a car.

4 Say that you shouted to try and stop him.

Vocabulary

die Polizei anrufen
was geschehen ist
an der Bushaltestelle
laut rufen
zum Halten bringen
telefonisch erreichen

Policeman

1 Ask his/her name and address.

2 Ask what happened.

3 Ask why the car did not stop more quickly.

4 Ask if he/she knows the little boy and where he lives.

   Thank him/her and ask for telephone number. Ask when
   he/she will be at home to receive a call.

Situation 34

You are in town, and in the street you see a friend whom you have not seen for some time. You go over and speak to him/her.

1   Ask how he/she is, and how his/her family are.

2   Ask why he/she hasn't been to see you for so long.

3   Suggest meeting soon.

4   Ask if he/she has time to come and have a quick drink with you now.

Vocabulary

sich sehen lassen
zusammenkommen
beschäftigt sein
Zeit haben

Friend

1 Say you are all well; what about his/her family?

2 Say you have been very busy with your new job. Why didn't he/she phone?

3 Accept, but where and when? Make suggestions if necessary (e.g. cinema, café).

4 Accept, but ask where you can go, as you haven't much time to spare.

Situation 35

You have just arrived in Germany on holiday when your car breaks down about 50 km from the coast. Another motorist stops, and you go to speak to him/her.

1 Say that you have broken down, but you don't know what is wrong.

2 Ask for help in changing the wheel as you have never done it before.

3 Ask if he/she knows a good restaurant nearby.

4 Thank him/her for helping, and offer to take him/her to a café for a drink.

Vocabulary

eine Panne haben
keine Ahnung
den Reifen wechseln
der Pneudefekt
das Hinterrad
der Ersatzreifen
das Werkzeug

Motorist

1 Say you think there is a puncture in one of the rear tyres.

2 Ask where the spare tyre and the tools are kept.

3 Say there is a good restaurant called 'Zur alten Post' in the next village, about 2 km further on.

Ask how much further he/she has to drive today.

4 Say you live nearby, and invite him/her to your house for a drink instead.

Situation 36

You are in a German town, and you want to go to a well-known shopping street. You are on foot, and you ask a passer-by for advice.

1   You ask the best way to get there: on foot, by bus, or by underground?

2   Ask how long it will take.

3   Choose a means of transport and ask for directions.

4   Repeat the directions. Say thank you, and ask if he/she knows the shops in that street.

Vocabulary

am besten
zu Fuß
erste Straße links, zweite rechts
sich interessieren für
das Geschenk

Passer-by

1 Say it depends whether he/she is in a hurry. It is quite a nice walk, but it is quicker by bus or underground.

2 Ten minutes by underground, a quarter of an hour by bus.

3 If bus: bus stop is opposite book shop just down the road. If underground: underground station is first left, then second right.

4 Say you know them fairly well, and ask what kind of shops he/she is interested in.

Say the shops are mostly small and expensive: good for buying perfume, presents, etc.

Situation 37

You are staying in a German town, and have arranged to visit a friend living in an outlying district. You have been waiting for a bus for a long time, but no bus has come. You approach a passer-by, and engage him/her in conversation.

1   Ask why there are no buses.

2   You are in a hurry. Ask how else you can get there.

3   Find out where the nearest phone box is so that you can ring your friend.

4   You do not know your friend's phone number. How can you find out?

Vocabulary

die Telefonzelle
streiken
ziemlich weit von hier
das Telefonbuch

Passer-by

1 The buses are on strike today. How long has he/she been waiting?

2 Suggest taxi or underground, but the underground is rather a long way away.

Find out exactly where he/she is going and what time he/she is due to arrive there.

3 There is no phone box in this street, but he/she could try the nearby café.

4 Ascertain he/she knows name and address of friend. Tell him/her to look in phone directory or ask someone in café to help.

At the railway station

Situation 38

You are on your way to stay with a German family in a small German town. You have just arrived at the railway station, and there is no-one at the station to meet you. You telephone the family, and one of your pen-friend's parents answers the phone.

1 Say you have just arrived at the station.

2 You caught the eight o'clock train as your plane arrived earlier than expected.

3 You tried to ring from the airport, but no-one answered.

4 How do you get to their house?

Vocabulary

ankommen
früher
einkaufen gehen
erkennen
anhaben

Father/mother

1 Express surprise at early arrival and ask for an explanation.

2 Why hadn't he/she let you know?

3 Nobody answered as you had all gone shopping.

4 Say you will come and fetch him/her in the car. How will you be able to recognise him/her? What is he/she wearing? Where will you find him/her?

Did he/she have a good journey?

What has he/she had to eat? Would he/she like to go into the cafeteria to have a drink as it will take you a quarter of an hour to get there.

Situation 39

You are at the taxi rank at a railway station in a German town. You have a lot of luggage, and want to go to the airport to catch the 9.30 a.m. plane to London. You speak to a taxi-driver.

1 Ask the taxi-driver if he is free.

2 Say you haven't much time to spare, and how long will it take?

3 Ask him to help you with your luggage.

4 Say you have to be in London before lunch in order to meet your parents.

Vocabulary

Sind Sie frei?
der Flughafen
abhängen von
der Koffer
rechtzeitig

Taxi-driver

1 Say yes and ask where he/she wants to go.

2 Say it depends on the traffic, but you usually do it in about half an hour.

Ask what time is the flight.

3 Ask which suitcases belong to him/her.

Comment on weight of cases, and ask how long he/she has been staying in Paris.

4 Ask if there is another flight that morning.

Say you will do your best to arrive in time.

At the travel agency

Situation 40

You are a German man/woman. You are in a German town and you want to visit friends in a town 250 km away with your children aged nine and three. You visit a travel agency to enquire about the journey and, if possible, to buy your tickets. You speak to the travel agent.

1 Ask if it is possible to travel by train.

2 If it is, ask if you need to change trains, and if there is an alternative way of travelling.

3 Ask how long the journey will take, and about departure times.

4 Ask how much it will cost.

Vocabulary

mit dem Zug
reisen
umsteigen
die Abfahrtszeit
die Fahrkarte
einfach
die Rückfahrkarte
zum halben Preis

Travel agent

1 Say it is possible, but there is no direct service.

2 Say there is a direct coach service. Which would he/she prefer?

3 By train it takes four hours. There are several trains a day. By coach it takes six hours, but there is only one coach a day, and it leaves at 10 a.m.

4 Ask how many travelling, and age of children. Single or return?

   If train: children under four travel free. Fares: Second class is DM 100,00 single. Return is double. Children aged four to eleven pay half.
   If coach: Fare is DM 85,00 single. Return is double. Children aged six to twelve pay half.

   Does he/she want to buy tickets now? Arrange payment.

Situation 41

You are spending your summer holiday in a German town
100 km from the coast, but decide you would like to spend
a few days at the seaside. You go to a travel agency to make
enquiries, and speak to the travel agent.

1   Ask which are the best seaside resorts within easy reach.

2   Ask about different kinds of accommodation.

3   Ask about the cheapest and quickest way of getting there.

4   Make arrangements for journey.

Vocabulary

der Badeort
die Unterkunft
der sandige Strand
die Pension
der Campingplatz
der Direktzug

Travel agent

1 Does he/she want a large sandy beach or an interesting town?

2 Does he/she want a hotel, boarding house, camp-site, etc.?

3 Depending upon which chosen, ask for more detailed requirements (number in party, length of stay, etc.), and offer to book.

Train is fastest and direct. Coach is cheaper but slower.

4 What day and time does he/she want to travel?

At the
Fremdenverkehrszentrale

Situation 42

You have just arrived in a German town, and you go to the
Fremdenverkehrszentrale for information. You speak to an
employee.

1   Ask for help in finding a hotel.

2   Ask what there is to do and see in the region.

3   Ask if there is a restaurant in the hotel and where there are
good restaurants in the town.

4   Ask if there is a cinema.

Vocabulary

die Umgebung
der Komfort
Wie lange?
Wieviele Personen?
der Aufenthalt
angenehm

Employee

1   Ask what kind of hotel (price, comfort, length of stay, number in party).

    Recommend 'Hotel zur schönen Aussicht'.

2   Ask what he/she is interested in, then suggest anything suitable (museum, swimming, etc.).

3   Offer a list of restaurants in the town.

4   Say there is no cinema here, only in the next town, which is 6 km away. Has he/she a car? If not, there are plenty of buses.

    Wish him/her a good stay.

Situation 43

Yor are visiting Germany with your family. You have a young child, and do not want too expensive a holiday. On arriving at a seaside town, you go to the *Fremdenverkehrszentrale* and speak to an employee.

1   Ask if you can have a plan of the town.

2   Ask for a list of hotels and some advice about the best places to stay.

3   Ask where the best shops are, and the best restaurants.

4   Ask about interesting places to visit and things to do.

Vocabulary

der Stadtplan
das Hotelverzeichnis
drei Sterne
Vollpension
Halbpension
der Supermarkt
das Geschäftszentrum
das Viertel
malerisch

Employee

1 Would he/she like a simple plan of the town which costs nothing, or a map of the region, including town plan, which costs DM 2,50?

2 Offer a hotel list. What are their requirements (3 star, 2 star, 1 star, etc., full/half board, near the sea, etc.)?

 Offer to telephone and make booking.

3 What kind of shops? (Supermarket outside town, new hypermarket with smart shops, old picturesque quarter with small shops, etc.)

 What kind of restaurant do they want?

4 How old is the child? Mention beach activities; boat excursions, sailing, tennis. In town: museum, gardens, cinema. Castle a few kilometres away. Is information required about any of these?

Situation 44

You are on holiday in Germany with your family, including your elderly aunt. You go to a town in Southern Germany and call at the *Fremdenverkehrszentrale*. You speak to an employee at the enquiry desk.

1 Ask about the availability of hotel accommodation.

2 Say that a lift is essential because of your aunt.

3 Ask them to telephone to make a booking for you.

4 Ask about restaurants in the locality.

Vocabulary

reservieren
der Fahrstuhl
die Tante
der See
der Berg
außerhalb der Stadt

Employee

1   Find out how many in party, length of stay, how they are travelling.

Ask what kind of accommodation required (full/half board, bath, shower, etc.).

2   Ask what grade of hotel required: only two-star hotels and above have lifts.

Do they want a view of the lake or of the mountains? In town or out of town?

3   You agree to telephone, but explain that some hotels may be full. Would they mind being separated, either on different floors of the same hotel or in different hotels?

4   Either offer a list of restaurants or recommend several different restaurants.

At the airport

Situation 45

It is 2.30 p.m. You are at a South German airport to meet a friend arriving from North Germany. You go to the informaton desk, and speak to the clerk there.

1 Ask what time the flight is due to arrive.

2 Ask what time coaches leave the airport to go to the city centre.

3 Ask if there has been a message for you.

4 Thank him/her and ask where coaches leave from.

Vocabulary

der Flug
die Stadtmitte
die Nachricht
der Treffplatz
die Haupthalle

Clerk

1 Say flight should arrive at 2.45 p.m., but it will be one hour late.

2 Coaches to city centre run every half hour.

3 Ask his/her name. Yes, there is a message. When asked, say friend doesn't want him/her to wait, but will contact him/her later to suggest new rendez-vous.

4 They wait just outside the entrance to the main hall. Can he/she see them?

Situation 46

You are at a large German airport, waiting to catch a plane back to London. You hear an announcement, but cannot understand it. You decide to ask a passenger waiting near you if he/she can explain.

1 Say that you could not understand the announcement. It was too fast.

2 Say that you are afraid of missing your plane.

3 Say that someone has told you it is foggy in London, and that your flight will probably be delayed.

4 Ask if he/she will tell you when the departure time of your plane is announced.

Vocabulary

die Durchsage
der Flug
verpassen
Verspätung haben
der Nebel
sich zerteilen

Passenger

1 Say that announcement was for passengers to Holland. Is that where he/she is going?

2 Which flight does he/she want to catch?

3 Say that you have just heard that the fog has cleared. Is the weather often bad in London?

Does he/she live in London? If not, where?

You will be staying in the centre of London. How can you get there from Heathrow Airport?

4 Ask about his/her stay in Germany. What did he/she enjoy most?

At Customs

Situation 47

You are going through Customs on your way home from a holiday. You speak to a Customs officer.

1 Say that you have nothing to declare.

2 Ask why you are having to wait so long, as you have a train to catch.

3 Ask whether he wants to look inside your suitcase.

4 Say that the case he is looking at is not yours.

Vocabulary

verzollen
der Koffer
durchsuchen
im Ausland
das Gepäckstück
der Fotoapparat
gehören

Customs officer

1   Didn't he/she buy anything abroad?

2   There is a lot of luggage to check. How many pieces of luggage has he/she?

3   Ask him/her to open a suitcase. Why are there five cameras in this suitcase?

4   Ask why he/she was carrying it if it does not belong to him/her.

Ask his/her name and ask him/her to go with you.

Situation 48

During a long holiday in Germany you go to Austria for a few days, and on returning to Germany, where you will be staying for another month, you go through the German Customs, and speak to a Customs officer.

1 Declare what you have bought in Austria.

2 Say where and when you bought your camera before going to Austria.

3 Ask how much you will have to pay for your extra bottles of wine.

4 Ask if you can pick up your suitcases and leave.

Vocabulary

Österreich
der Tabak
der Wein
das Parfum
die Armbanduhr
Zoll zahlen
die Flasche

Customs officer

1 Ask if that is everything. Mention anything that may have been forgotten – wine, perfume, tobacco, etc.

2 Check that the watch he/she is wearing is not new.

3 Say the duty will be DM 2,00 a bottle. Ask how many extra bottles.

4 Check on which luggage belongs to him/her before allowing to pass.

At the camp-site

Situation 49

You are camping in Germany with your family, and your younger sister falls ill. You are the only member of the family who speaks German, so you have to speak to the doctor when he arrives.

1 Say your sister is feeling unwell.

2 Say you think it is something she ate yesterday.

3 Say she slept very badly last night, and she seems feverish.

4 Say your parents are very worried, and ask if you should go back home.

Vocabulary

sich nicht wohl fühlen
etwas Schlechtes gegessen haben
Fieber haben
sich Sorgen machen
nach Hause zurückkehren
Schmerzen haben
die Temperatur messen
Zimmer in einem Hotel nehmen

Doctor

1 Ask what the trouble is. Has she a pain, and if so, where?

2 Ask what she had to eat yesterday, and if she has eaten
anything today.

3 Ask if her temperature has been taken.

Ask how old she is and if she is often ill.

4 Say that it isn't necessary to go home. It's nothing serious,
but she needs rest. Could they perhaps move to a hotel?

Situation 50

You are on holiday in Germany with your family, and you are the only one who speaks German. You have just arrived at a camp-site. You go to the camp office, and speak to the employee there.

1 Say who you are, and that you have booked for a week.

2 Ask where you can put up your tent.

3 Ask if you can buy fresh bread and milk on the site.

4 Ask where the toilets and showers are.

Vocabulary

einen Platz reservieren
das Zelt aufschlagen
die Dusche
sonst noch etwas

At the post office

Employee

1 Check on how booking was made, and on people in family.

2 Say that it isn't far, and that you will accompany them.

3 Say there is milk in camp shop, and baker delivers bread at eight o'clock every morning. Ask if he/she would prefer to shop at the nearest supermarket. If so, does he/she know where it is?

4 Toilets and showers are 25 metres away, on the right.

   Is there anything else they want to know?

At the post office

Situation 51

While on holiday in Germany, you go into a post office, and speak to the counter clerk.

1 Ask how much the postage is to England.

2 Ask for four stamps, and ask how long it takes for a letter to get to England.

3 Say that you have a parcel to send to England.

4 Ask if you can borrow a pen to fill in the form, and ask how much it costs.

Vocabulary

die Briefmarke
das Päckchen
das Formular
ausfüllen
die Ansichtskarte
der Inhalt
der Wert
die Zolldeklaration

Counter clerk

1 Ask whether it is for letters or postcards, and give the rates.

2 Say a letter takes only a few days, but a postcard takes about a week.

3 Ask about the contents and value of the parcel, and ask him/her to fill in a form for the Customs.

4 Say the parcel plus stamps comes to DM 10,50.

Situation 52

You are travelling in Germany, and have arranged for your family to send letters for you to collect at the local post office. You go to the post office, and speak to the counter clerk.

1 Ask whether there is any mail for you.

2 Ask whether there will be another delivery today, as you are expecting another letter.

3 Buy stamps for the letters and postcards you have to post.

4 You have a parcel to post.

Vocabulary

die Postzustellung
erwarten
der Personalausweis
später wieder kommen
das Ausland

Counter clerk

1 Ask what name. There is one letter. Ask for identification.

2 There will be another delivery later in the day. Ask if he/she can call back.

   Ask how long he/she will be staying.

3 How many letters? How many postcards? Where are they going to?

4 Where is the parcel going? There is a Customs declaration to fill in if it is going out of the country. What is in the parcel, and what is its value?

At the police station

Situation 53

You are staying with a family in Germany. You have lost your purse, but are not sure where you have lost it. You go to the local police station and speak to a policeman.

1 Ask if he can help you as you have lost your purse.

2 Give a description of the purse and its contents (money and air ticket to London).

3 Say that you have to go back to England in a few days' time and don't know what to do.

4 Ask what you should do about your lost air ticket.

Vocabulary

verlieren
das Portemonnaie
das Flugticket
die Münze
das Fundbüro
wenig Aussicht

Policeman

1 Ask where and when it was lost.

2 Ask what enquiries have been made so far, i.e. shops, transport, etc.

3 Suggest he/she goes to the Lost Property Office.

   Ask for details of the German family as they could send the purse on to England if it is found.

4 Suggest he/she telephones the airport to explain about the air ticket.

   Say that you will do your best to find the purse, but you are not very hopeful.

Situation 54

You are staying in a German town when you discover that you have lost your wallet which contained nearly all your money. You go to the police station to report the loss, and speak to a policeman.

1 Tell him about losing your wallet.

2 Say you have lost nearly all your money and that you don't know what to do.

3 Ask him if he has any suggestions to make.

4 Say that you will have to go home sooner than you had intended.

Vocabulary

die Brieftasche
vorschlagen
der Reisepaß
die Britische Botschaft
das Scheckbuch
der Reisescheck
das Reisebüro
die Versicherung

Policeman

1 Sympathise and find out exactly when and where it was lost, and what he/she has done about it. Establish contents of wallet.

2 Has he/she still got passport and airline tickets? If yes, say there should be no problem. If no, suggest he/she contact British Embassy and airline.

3 Ask if he/she has a credit card or a cheque book, or any travellers' cheques. If yes, suggest going to a bank. If no, suggest phoning family or contacting British Empassy.

4 Ask if insured. If so, suggest going to travel agency to make claim.

Staying in a German family

Situation 55

**You are staying with a German family by the name of Krüger.
You go into the kitchen and speak to Herr/Frau Krüger.**

1 Ask if you can help with the washing up.

2 Say that you are enjoying your stay very much and hope that
   he/she isn't too tired with the extra work.

3 Say that you want to do some shopping in town. Is there
   anything he/she needs from the shops?

4 Ask what time you need to be back for lunch.

Vocabulary

helfen
abwaschen
Mühe machen
in die Stadt
zu Mittag
das Geschirrtuch

Herr/Frau Krüger

1 Thank him/her. Does he/she know where the tea-towel is?

2 What does he/she do to help at home?

  You're not too tired, and it's a pleasure having him/her. Would he/she like to come again next year?

3 Does he/she know where the baker's is, as you would like some bread and cakes.

4 Lunch is at 12.30. Don't be late, as you will be going out in the car later. Would he/she like to come?

Situation 56

You are in Germany, staying with a German family. They have all gone out, leaving you alone, as you wanted to write a letter. The telephone rings and you answer it.

1 Ask who it is.

2 Say where everybody has gone.

3 Ask if you can take a message, or if the caller would prefer to ring back.

4 Say what time the family will probably be back.

Vocabulary

Wer spricht, bitte?
etwas ausrichten
etwas vorhaben
einladen

Caller

1 Say it is Herr or Frau Grün, and ask to speak to Herr or Frau Hell.

Ask who is speaking.

2 Ask why he/she has been left alone in the house.

3 Ask if he/she knows what the family has planned for Saturday evening, as you would like to invite them to dinner. Would he/she like to come too?

Ask if he/she is enjoying the stay, and how much longer he/she will be in Germany,

4 Will he/she ask Herr or Frau Hell to phone when they return?

Situation 57

You have been staying with a German family, and you would like to buy them a present before you go home. You discuss this with a friend.

1   Ask if he/she has any ideas about a suitable present.

2   Say you have DM 25,00 to spend.

3   Find out where the best shops are.

4   Ask if he/she will come and help you choose something.

Vocabulary

das Geschenk
passend
die Pralinen (*pl.*)
das Spielzeug
das Spiel
das Kaufhaus

Friend

1 Ask if they all like chocolates. If yes, say you know where to buy delicious chocolates. If no, suggest flowers, or toys for the children. What do they like to play with?

2 Say little cars and some games are not expensive.

3 The best shops are the department stores in the town centre. When will he/she have time to go there?

4 Agree, but you can only manage a lunch hour. Will that be all right? If so, arrange to meet.

At the bank

Situation 58

You are in a bank in Germany, and speak to the bank clerk.

1 Ask if you can change some English money into German DM.

2 Ask what is the rate of exchange.

3 Ask if you can use your credit card in Germany.

4 Ask where the cash desk is.

Vocabulary

Geld wechseln
der Wechselkurs
die Kreditkarte
der Kassenschalter
sich ausweisen
bar zahlen
Schlange stehen

Bank clerk

1   He/she can change money if he/she has proof of identity.

2   Give the current rate. How much does he/she want to change?

3   In many places it is possible: look for the sign. But it is often cheaper to pay cash.

4   On his/her right, where there is a queue.

Ask how long he/she is staying in Germany, what visits he/she has made, etc.

At home

Situation 59

You go into the living room at home, where your mother/father is working, and speak to him/her.

1 Say that you are going to see a friend.

2 Say that if anyone phones you will be at Sylvie's house.

3 Ask what time dinner will be ready.

4 Ask what is for dinner.

Vocabulary

anrufen
fertig
die Schulaufgabe
das Brathähnchen
das Gemüse

Mother/father

1 Has he/she finished homework?

2 Who is he/she expecting to phone?

Who is Sylvie?

3 Dinner will be ready at 7.30 p.m. Can he/she be home by 7 p.m., as you will need some help?

4 Chicken for dinner, but you haven't yet decided what vegetables. What would he/she like?

On holiday in Germany

Situation 60

**You are on holiday in Germany, and have run short of money.
You decide to ask a German friend for help.**

1 Say that you have telephoned your parents to ask them to send you some more money.

2 Ask if you can borrow some money.

3 Say you will pay back the loan when the money arrives from your parents.

4 Apologise for having to ask for money.

Vocabulary

bitten um
leihen
zurückzahlen
Geld abheben